KATHERINE ATWELL HERBERT

THE PERFECT SCREENPLAY

Writing It and Selling It

ALLWORTH PRESS
NEW YORK

10   09   08   07   06   5   4   3   2   1

Published by Allworth Press
An imprint of Allworth Communications, Inc.
10 East 23rd Street, New York, NY 10010

Cover design by Derek Bacchus
Interior design by Mary Belibasakis
Typography by Integra Software Services
Cover photo: © Corbis

ISBN: 1-58115-439-9

Library of Congress Cataloging-in-Publication Data:

Herbert, Katherine Atwell.
   The perfect screenplay/Katherine Atwell Herbert.
      P.   cm.
   Includes index.
1. Motion picture authorship.   2. Motion picture authorship—Marketing.   I. Title.

PN1996.H428 2005
808.2'3—dc22

                                                                                    2005035238

Printed in Canada

Dedication

To Stephen Tod, Amy Elizabeth,
and Jill Anne, just because

CONTENTS

Part 111 Looking Like a Pro

Part 1V Destination Hollywood